YOUR ONE WEEK
COUNTDOWN TO A
BRILLIANT
PRESENTATION

Hazel Walker

Published by Pink Office Publishing

© Hazel Walker 2011

Hazel Walker asserts the moral right to be
identified as the author of this work.

Printed in Great Britain by Walkerreed Limited
Chelmsford. Bound by Hipwells, Maldon.

ISBN 978-9568150-0-2

Other titles in the series include YOUR ONE WEEK COUNTDOWN TO...

BRILLIANT MOTIVATION

Lost your mojo? Can't get yourself going? Here's the answer to your lack of motivation: get your mojo working and, very important, keep it going when you need it most.

£9.99

BRILLIANT ASSERTIVENESS

Discover effective and elegant ways of communicating and watch your confidence soar as a result of using these tried and tested assertiveness techniques.

£9.99

BRILLIANT CONFIDENCE

Boost your confidence whenever you need to with these simple, practical exercises and activities, and discover how to keep your confidence at an all-time high.

£9.99

BRILLIANT TIME MANAGEMENT

Take control of your life and realise your dreams. Sounds too simple? It IS simple with these proven time management techniques and activities.

£9.99

Introduction

You can deliver a brilliant presentation with just one week to prepare. That's a promise. If you follow the exercises and activities in this book and use the tools it provides, you will do it.

Believe this, and you're on your way. In fact, if you need to crunch seven days down to, say, two or three, you could still give a perfectly good presentation, without any problem.

I make two assumptions here: one is that you know your subject. If you're planning a 30-minute presentation on Outer Mongolia in seven days' time and you know nothing about the place, this book probably won't help much. I doubt any book can help you. Knowledge and the information you want to share are, of course, vital elements of your presentation.

But if you know your subject reasonably well and just need to put your knowledge in order, wrap it up into a logical presentation and deliver it with confidence, you're going to be fine.

The other assumption I make is that you know how to create a Power Point presentation. I don't teach Power Point, but there are dozens of YouTube clips on it, or contact my friend Katherine Davison at www.epiphany training.co.uk and let her show you how to do a really professional slide show.

I coach men and women who are literally speechless with fright at the prospect of standing up in front of people and saying something.

I have always succeeded in helping them and, if you use the tools I provide in this book, I'll help you.

My method is tried and tested and it works. The reason it works so well, I believe, is that I encourage you to work on two aspects of your presentation.

While we will of course be working on the material you are going to present, we'll also work on **you**, on managing your nervousness and on building your confidence. Over the seven days of activities in this book, you'll focus equally on the presentation and on yourself. Of course, if you have longer than a week in which to prepare, that's great, and you can devote as much time and energy as you like to getting yourself and your presentation ready. But one week is enough, if that's all the time you have available to you.

If you're prepared to devote around 60 minutes a day to your preparation, for just one week, I guarantee you will deliver a brilliant presentation.

Preparing not only your material but yourself means I will help you to engage with one of your most powerful weapons, your subconscious. If you've always dreaded having to deliver a speech or a presentation, your subconscious has spent years, perhaps decades, setting in concrete a rock-solid foundation of (completely unfounded) belief that says "I'm no good at presentations".

During the week to come, we'll be doing some very effective and spectacularly successful work on banishing those old negative thoughts.

We will also engage your subconscious to help you make sure everything is in place when you need it.

This book will give you everything you need to build up to the big day so that you can start out feeling confident and calm and in control.

**Trust me — or, more importantly,
trust *yourself*.**

If you have time, please read through the whole book before your week begins so there are no surprises.

Remember, you'll need around an hour a day, maybe more if you have a longer presentation or if you're especially nervous. Look on the time you devote to preparation as an investment in your own wellbeing. You'll benefit from the efforts you make not just in terms of the presentation but in every area of your life.

Use the blank pages at the end of each chapter for your own notes and ideas, and do refer back to them after you've delivered your presentation. Every activity and exercise in this book is designed to encourage you to think positively and, perhaps, differently about yourself, your presentation and the way you deliver it, so my hope is that you will develop your own ideas and activities as you go along.

With one positive change under your belt, my hope is that you'll want to make even more and bigger changes in your life. That's my mission, after all — to enable people to live their best lives.

Whether this is your one and only dip in the pool of personal development, or the beginning of an ongoing quest to live your best life, this one-week investment of your time and energy will repay huge dividends. I know you will be delighted with the result.

And once you've made one good presentation, there'll be no stopping you.

Enjoy the journey.

> — Hazel Walker
> redbird coaching

CONTENTS

Pink Office Publishing is the trading name of
Hazel Walker Limited, registered in England
No. 05648091, 93 Burlescoombe Road, SS1 3PT

DAY ONE
Start with some homework

*Make a start on preparing your
material and <u>see</u> yourself doing well*

L et's start by laying down some simple ground rules. First, everything you'll do this week as a result of reading this book will be firmly fixed within the framework of my *Four Laws of Presentations*, which are over the page. We will be referring to them throughout this book, and if you obey them you won't put a foot wrong.

Second, while you'll love most of the activities and exercises I'll ask you to do this week, some of them may require some hard thinking on your part and some might, perhaps, make you feel a little uncomfortable. Please

DAY ONE

commit to working through them, especially if you find them testing. It's the testing stuff that will make the most difference!

Third, please allocate at least one hour a day to preparation of your presentation and yourself. Depending on your previous experience, the length and complexity of the presentation and your level of nervousness, you may need to spend more than one hour on some days: make sure you can fit this time into your schedule.

So, here for the first but by no means the last time, are my

FOUR LAWS OF PRESENTATIONS

1. PREPARE: do your homework on both yourself and your topic

2. PLAN: start with the end in mind. Visualise yourself and your audience having a great time

3. PRODUCE: your speech in its entirety and then as "prompts".

4. PRACTISE: practise, practise and then practise some more

Let's start with the basics, the preparation of your material. Think about this: if you were an actor taking on a major role you would spend weeks, perhaps months, preparing for your role with rehearsals and run-throughs. Imagine yourself, then, as the lead player in a new drama – your presentation – and prepare accordingly. Your preparation needs to be even more intense than the actor's in some ways, because you need to respond to audience interaction, questions and distractions in a way the actor doesn't.

> **Practise being self-aware, so that
> you can recognise and address what
> nervousness does to you.**

It takes different people in different ways. Find the best way for YOU to address your nerves. There's lots of help with this later in this chapter.

You will need to know your topic like the back of your hand, and from all possible angles, so start by making sure you know your stuff, then try to see it from your audience's point of view, and do some more research until you are confident that you have a good 360° view of your subject.

Can you chat about it with someone you feel comfortable with for, say,

10 minutes, without having to look something up or check your figures? If you were to be asked questions on your subject, could you field them comfortably?

It's at this point that people begin to panic, so first of all take a couple of deep breaths and remember that this book is going to help you to succeed in making this presentation brilliant. Now, you need to be very clear what the point of your presentation is.

What is it that you want your audience to know after your presentation that they didn't know before?

If you can't answer this question simply, in no more than a couple of sentences, you may need to reconsider your subject matter.

My presentation coaching clients often come to me with a hugely inflated idea of what they're going to convey to their audience, and this is usually because they are so nervous about the whole business that they've thrown in everything, including the kitchen sink.

There's no need. Simple is good. Don't try to cram too much into one presentation – much better to break a large amount of material, or complex ideas, into two or three presentations rather than trying to cram too much information into one complicated one. Think about your presentation from your audience's point of view and don't overload them.

Think about how you can hold on to your audience's attention.

There's no such thing as "the average attention span" because it varies from person to person and subject to subject. One person may find it easy to focus on one subject for hours while he can only concentrate on another for a few minutes at a time.

As a rule of thumb, think about changing pace or introducing a different view or new aspect of your presentation, or an activity, every 15 minutes or so. We'll work more on keeping your audience interested and changing pace on Day Three.

Do you need props or visual aids of any kind to help illustrate what you're saying?

And can you create Power Point slides that will really add something to what you're saying?

Once you've clearly defined what it is you want your audience to know, jot down some bullet point notes on the areas you will cover to get your message across. There are blank pages at the end of each chapter for your notes.

> A word on Power Point: never, repeat, never put your whole presentation on slides and read them aloud. This is an insult to your audience who can, presumably, read; it also tends to mean you're delivering a lazy presentation. Don't doom your audience to "death by Power Point". Your Power Point slides should add something to what you say, or illustrate a point, or build on an idea you've introduced. Be rigorous: if you can't honestly say a slide is building on what you're saying, leave it out.

Remember, you need to be clear about what you want your audience to know once you've finished speaking. With that in your mind, it's straightforward to simply jot down a word or phrase to represent each part of what you want to say. What we're looking for initially is a sort of brain dump, everything you need to say, in bullet point form. You might want to make a list, create a mind map, or do a more structured analysis of your subject matter. Whatever works for you is fine. Spend some time fleshing out your list of bullet points until you feel confident that they include at least paragraph headings of everything you're going to say.

Now you have "the meat" of your presentation, and I'm going to give you the perfect recipe, in the form of three simple steps, to make sure your audience will feel completely satisfied by what you dish up.

This three-step foolproof structure was whispered to me by the senior lecturer in my department just before I stepped in front of a classroom full of students for the very first time.

> **"Don't forget," he said, "Tell 'em**
> **what you're gonna tell 'em, tell 'em,**
> **then tell 'em what you've told 'em".**

It became a kind of mantra that I've never forgotten and have used for lectures in schools and colleges, before I speak in public to an audience large or small, for workshops and seminars, at Toastmasters... in fact, anywhere I need to get a message across. It never fails me. It applies to every presentation – formal, informal, long, short, educational, comedic, dramatic, you name it, this structure applies.

DAY ONE

Foolproof Presentation Formula

Step One: Tell them what you're going to tell them. That is, introduce your subject and give your audience a brief summary of what it is and what they will know by the time you've finished.

So for example, if your presentation is called "My Cleaning Company Gives the Best Service" you could start with something like "Good afternoon everyone, welcome to the world of excellent cleaning. I'm Fred Bloggs, and I'm going to give you 15 good reasons why My Cleaning is the best in the market."

That's it, that's about as much as you need to say in an introduction. Don't tie yourself in knots trying to sound posh, don't cram too much in. Keep it simple.

You'll probably need to use one Power Point slide for this, giving your name and your details, probably showing your company logo and perhaps the title of the presentation, a kind of business card if you like.

Step Two: Tell them. That is, say what you have to say about your subject. This is the meat of your presentation, where you pass on all your good information so that your audience will know what you want them to know by the time you've finished.

At this stage, all you need are the bullet points, the top level notes on what you're going to talk about. We'll pull them together and put them into a sensible order over the next day or so but for now, you just need to have your bullet points ready.

As a rule of thumb, you will probably want one Power Point slide for each bullet point. If your presentation is going to take 30 minutes, aim at having around 12 Power Point slides: one for the introduction, 10 for the meat, one for the finale.

For the My Cleaning Company example, you would have one slide for your introduction, then you could probably fit two or more reasons on each slide, illustrating or fleshing out what you're saying, and one or possibly two to close, see Step Three.

Step Three: Tell them what you've told them. That is, summarise what you've said, so that you can drive home your message, whatever it is.

To go back to the Cleaning Company example, you might say

something like: "So those are my 15 great reasons, and I hope you can see that my company really shines when it comes to excellent service. We pride ourselves on being the premiere cleaning company in Anyville, and if you'd like to know more, I'm happy to answer your questions."

Again, keep it simple, brief, to the point. One or perhaps two wrap-up slides could list your 15 good reasons again, or perhaps you could use pictures representing your good reasons.

Spend some time thinking about your subject matter, your bullet point notes, and the big question: *what is it you want your audience to know when you've finished speaking?*

Decide the best way to fit your material into the three steps of the Foolproof Presentation Formula, bearing in mind the time available and the subject you're covering.

At this stage, all you can do is an estimate of the time you'll need to cover your subject: if you're aiming at 45 minutes, and your estimate at the moment looks as though you can only fill 20, go back and do some more brainstorming. Or think about how you can add examples or illustrations or perhaps tell a story which will help you to drive home some of your main points.

Consider audience interaction: will it help you to open the floor for questions? You will need to feel completely confident about your subject to do this: you ought to be able to think through all possible angles, and all possible questions, and feel happy with your responses. You also need to bear in mind you will need to be firm about how long you can spend on the questions generated.

Could you give your audience an activity to carry out? If it will definitely add something to their understanding of your subject, fine. Otherwise, leave it out.

Arrange your notes in what feels like a good order. That's as much as you need to do on your material today. Easy, huh?

N ow please start on getting yourself ready by doing some **visualisation**. If you've ever attended one of my workshops or seminars, you'll know I'm a big fan of visualisation and I hope you will be too by the time you've used it once or twice successfully. Start by relaxing; find somewhere comfortable to settle and give yourself half an hour or so of uninterrupted peace – believe me, this half hour investment now will pay huge dividends later. Now close your eyes and conjure up, in your mind, a vivid image of yourself delivering your presentation. SEE yourself standing in front of your audience, calm and focused; see the audience looking fascinated and enthused by what you're saying.

At the end of your presentation, see
the audience clapping or cheering
you as you take your leave.

See everyone smiling and looking completely satisfied and contented. Fill in as many details as you can so that you have a mini-movie in your mind: you, your presentation, your enthralled audience.

Now run this mini-movie again and again, making the images more vivid each time you run it; make the colours brighter, make the sounds clearer – hear your voice explaining the most difficult part of your presentation with consummate ease. Hear your audience clapping you at the end. See their smiles. See your own smile. Feel what you'll feel as your audience gives you a standing ovation. What you're doing by creating this mini-movie is using a technique that sportsmen and women and athletes use all the time.

Athlete Roger Bannister used visualisation to prepare himself for his record-breaking sub-four-minute mile.

> **He wrote "3:58" on a slip of paper and**
> **put it in his running shoe,**
> **visualising it every time he ran.**

When he wasn't running, he'd visualise himself running. He gradually shaved second after second off his time until he achieved the "impossible" sub-four-minute mile on May 6 1954.

The great Jack Canfield, one of my favourite motivational speakers and writers, and author of *The Success Principles* (among others), tells a marvellous story of what was basically a visualisation party. He and all the other guests were asked to attend *as they would be* in five years' time.

One of the happy partygoers was starting out as a writer and arrived carrying mock-ups of three bestselling books she "had written".
This was something of a stretch at the time since, at that particular moment, she'd never sold a single book. Five years on though, that

partygoer, whose name was Susan Jeffers, could boast of having written the book that gave her international acclaim and a long-standing place in the bestseller lists, *Feel The Fear And Do It Anyway*. She has written another 16 critically acclaimed and hugely successful books since then.

Jack Nicklaus, who earned millions during his long career as a professional golfer, won trophies and cups galore and is regarded as one of the greats of his generation.

> **He always used visualisation. He says:**
> **"I never hit a shot, not even in practice,**
> **without having a very sharp, in-focus**
> **picture of it in my head.**

"First I see the ball where I want it to finish, nice and white and sitting up high on the bright green grass.

"Then the scene quickly changes, and I see the ball going there; its path, trajectory, and shape, even its behaviour on landing. Then there is a sort of fade-out, and the next scene shows me making the kind of swing that will turn the previous images into reality."

Why we mere humans don't use visualisation more in our everyday lives is a complete mystery to me. It's easy, it's enjoyable, a little like controlled daydreaming, it certainly can't do any harm, and it's free. It's also incredibly powerful and effective. Use it now to give you a wonderfully effective boost in preparing you for delivering a brilliant presentation. It's especially important to use positive visualisation if you've always dreaded presentations: you have probably subconsciously visualised yourself floundering in front of an audience many times, so it's vital that you offset all that negative input with a fully positive mind-movie.

If you find it difficult to visualise at first, please persevere. Think of it as nothing more than controlled daydreaming: that's really all it is. Relax, focus on the images you want to develop, and let your mind create a perfectly positive outcome. Enjoy!

Your notes

DAY TWO

Plan to succeed

Put your presentation in order and
gear yourself up for the big day

Y ou've made a start on preparing your subject matter and, incidentally, you've flagged to your subconscious that you need lots of information on that subject. Today, as well as building on your earlier preparation for the presentation, you're going to continue the important work you began yesterday which focused on preparing *yourself*.

First of all, let's just focus on your material for a few minutes. Run your eyes over your subject matter bullet points and see if you need to add

DAY TWO

anything; your subconscious will have started getting very busy on your behalf by now, so you'll find you have more info to add to your bullet point notes and can start to put them into logical order.

Decide whether you have everything you need to be convincing. If you need to do any more research, do it today and collect together all the material available to you.

Do you need statistics or evidence to prove your points? Can you give examples to clarify what you're saying? What visual aids will you use? Think about how you can change pace and perhaps direction in your presentation so that you can keep your audience interested.

Write each of your bullet point paragraphs on a separate sheet of paper and arrange them in a logical order. You may need to re-order them — that's fine.

We'll do some more work on your material tomorrow.

Today's the day to contact the venue and make sure everything is ready for you: laptop, projector, screen; tables or desks, preferably one on each side of the presentation area so that you can use visual aids to remind you to move around. It's also worth double-checking that your audience is actually expecting the subject matter you're working on; keep in mind that what's obvious to you may not be quite so blindingly obvious to everyone else.

One of my presentation coaching clients, I'll call him Bill Smith, came to me with his own sorry story about mixed messages: he had delivered an excellent presentation at his large, multinational company's annual conference called Skills In The 21st Century Workplace, all about how staff need a broader range of skills now than ever before. On the agenda, Bill's speaking slot looked like this:

10am **Presentation** Skills In the 21st Century Workplace *by Bill Smith.*

A few weeks passed and he received an invitation from a regional manager to deliver his "excellent" presentation to colleagues in the north. He agreed, and it was only by chance that he discovered, the day before he was due to head north, that the regional manager had misunderstood the listing and was expecting Bill to deliver a rousing speech on Presentation Skills. The regional manager hadn't noticed the fact that "Presentation" was in bold type, signifying that this part of the agenda wasn't a "Discussion" or a "Feedback". It was a simple misinterpretation,

DAY TWO

but left Bill in a terrible pickle which would have been even worse if he hadn't taken the trouble to check was what expected of him.

Always check and double check that everyone is, as they say, reading from the same hymn-sheet.

You need to start thinking now about how you will remind yourself to move around during your presentation: movement will make you look and feel much more relaxed. If you stand rigidly still, your frozen body language will make your audience uncomfortable and will cause you to tense up.

So moving around is vital, and if you don't do it naturally, use whatever props are to hand to help you. Put some of your visual aids, if you have them, on a table or desk on one side of the presentation area, and perhaps a jug of water and some glasses on the other. No visual aids? That's fine – put a set of felt tips next to a flip chart on one side of you and your water on the other side.

You may or may not be using the flip chart or white board, but having it in place will remind you that you need to move around once you've started speaking. It's absolutely fine to pause and take a drink of water during your presentation, by the way: everyone's mouth tends to dry up through nervousness, so be willing to acknowledge this and make sure there's water available and, more to the point, DRINK it!

A word about visual aids: unless you're delivering a "show and tell", don't be tempted to use visual aids that have to be passed round – this will only distract your audience from you and what you're saying. Visual aids need to be big enough to be seen by everyone at the same time but small enough to be manageable. If in doubt, take a picture and include it in your Power Point presentation.

Today is also the day to decide what you're going to wear. This may sound trivial, but it can mean the difference on the Big Day between you feeling comfortable and confident or uncomfortable and uncertain about what you're going to say.

You don't have to have new clothes, but you do have to have a clean, well pressed, well presented outfit that's suitable for the venue and subject matter. You need to be able to put your outfit on, know that you look well groomed, and then forget about how you look. If you need a haircut, get it done today or tomorrow; if your best suit needs cleaning, take it to the dry cleaners' today and make a note to collect it in good time; polish your shoes really thoroughly today so that they'll only need a bit of a shine-up on the day.

Check that you have all the bits and pieces necessary to complete your outfit, whatever it is: cufflinks, scarf, tie, jewellery, shirt, blouse, tights, socks etc etc.

**Try on your outfit and check it out
in front of a full-length mirror.**

Making sure your outfit works and is appropriate is such a simple thing to do but it's often overlooked in the run-up to a presentation. "It's my message that's important, not the way I look," my clients sometimes say, and I agree...but with a proviso. It's true it doesn't matter how you look, so long as you and your outfit don't detract from the message you're trying to convey. Years ago, I attended a seminar called, ironically as it turned out, "Dress for Success" and while I can't remember a thing about the content,

I vividly remember the presenter's awful, crumpled, ill-fitting sack of a dress. Why she hadn't taken on board her own ideas and dressed well for the occasion, I have no idea. But it was a big mistake.

I was mesmerised by the woman's tragically inappropriate look, as was the rest of the audience. Afterwards, the buzz around the room was not about what she'd said, but about what she'd worn.

To avoid the audience drifting off into a world of wonderment about what you're wearing, make sure your look is:

 comfortable without being casual: you will be aware of the kind of clothes your audience is going to be wearing and if you're not, find out. If you're addressing a black tie event, for example, you absolutely must conform. Likewise, if you're running a lunchtime workshop for a team-building within a company, wear suitable clothes that enable you to fit into the environment.

appropriate for the venue.

appropriate for your subject matter

well groomed.

Once your outfit is settled, take a long hard look at yourself in a full-length mirror and check your posture. If you stand tall, you will not only look slimmer and taller, your breathing will improve and you will give subtle body language signals that say "hey, I'm someone who knows what I'm talking about".

Your posture and your body language is doubly powerful in making you feel confident. First off, people will respond to you as though you are a confident, calm, in-control person if that's what your body language says.

And secondly, by adopting confident body language you send a clear message to your subconscious, saying "I'm confident. I'm feeling good. I'm in control. I'm calm."

Once the message has sunk in, your subconscious will very obligingly do everything possible to make your message true. Your subconscious will filter out anything that suggests you are not confident, and will allow into your consciousness all the signs and signals that say yes, you are confident. If it helps, think about someone you know or someone you've seen on tv or in a film who is supremely confident and copy their body language and posture. Start doing this now, before the big day, so that it becomes second nature to you and there's no hint of awkwardness or embarrassment. It may feel strange at first, but it definitely works, so it's worth persevering.

Check your body language and correct your posture now, today, and check it out every time you pass a mirror or a shop window from now on. It's simple: stand straight, with your shoulders back and down, head held high, relax. Imagine you have a piece of string attached to the very top of your head that's pulling you gently upwards so you walk tall.

Let's get this out in the open: you are going to be nervous on the day, and there's no point pretending otherwise. Even the most experienced presenters and the most famous actors get nervous before they go on.

The difference between the brilliant presenters and actors and the rest is that the brilliant ones acknowledge their nervousness, know how to manage it, and actually use it to improve their performance.

So I want you to think about how you can deal with your nerves and start today practising how you'll cope. You may already have some tried and tested methods of dealing with nervousness and if so, great, start practising them straight away.

If you don't already have some calmers, here are four simple ones. Remember, there's absolutely nothing wrong with feeling nervous before your presentation. The key is to know how to deal with that nervousness.

Try these solutions out now, while you're not nervous, and practise them regularly over the next few days so that when the time comes you remember what to do. Use all of them if you can, or just choose those with which you feel most comfortable.

Manage your nervousness - 1

There are three steps to this exercise, but they're easy, and they don't take long.

When you're nervous, your breathing tends to be faster and shallower than normal. You can calm yourself down in a matter of seconds by doing this simple three by three exercise:

i **Think of a clear blue sky.** Concentrate on the vivid blue. No clouds, just a clear bright blue. Close your eyes if you can and if it's appropriate. If you've practised this enough, you'll be able to picture your blue sky in your mind even with your eyes open.

ii **Take a good deep breath** – breathe in through your nose to a count of one-elephant-two-elephant-three-elephant-four-elephant-five, out through your mouth to a count of one-elephant-two-elephant-three-elephant-four-elephant-five. Do this three times.

iii **Repeat step two twice more**, so that altogether you've taken nine deep breaths. This will take you no longer than a minute or so as you'll realise when you practise this in a non-threatening situation. Notice, too, how much calmer you feel. Take one more deep breath for luck. Lift your chin and smile.

Manage your nervousness - 2

Take a time out. If it's feasible, leave the room, or move away from whatever is making you feel panicky. Simply changing your position can help you to get past a sudden bout of nervousness.

Give yourself some space with a mental breather. Say something in your head like "I can take this slowly" or "I'm calming myself" or "Let's calm right down".

DAY TWO

Use whatever form of words feels right for you. Taking this moment will bring your panic level down a notch; the fact that you're taking a measure of control will help too.

Once you've bought yourself some time, take three deep breaths, then three more. Now you're ready to face the music.

Manage your nervousness - 3

Another exercise with three simple steps, a good one to do before you start your presentation. Stretch if you have room and it's appropriate:

i Raise your arms up high over your head, reaching up a little higher than you think you can. Feel the stretch through your spine and across your shoulders.

ii Step back on one foot then lean forward, bending from the waist, feeling the stretch down the back of the back leg. Change legs and repeat.

iii Put your right arm up, bend at the elbow, then reach as far down your back with your right hand as you can. Push gently with the other hand. Repeat on the other side.

Naturally, you'll only be able to do these stretches if there's time and a suitable place. Once you've actually started speaking, try...

Manage your nervousness - 4

Anything that buys you a little time, once you're on stage, is good. If you've practised deep breathing, that's the easiest and one of the most effective calmers, but you can develop your own calming exercises, and choose whatever works best for you. Take a long drink of water, for example, focusing on the cool feel in your mouth and throat, following, in your mind's eye if you can, the course the water takes down into your stomach. While your mind's eye is turned inward, take two or three deep breaths and do a mini visualisation of yourself delivering a really inspiring presentation. If you practise a mini visualisation every time you take a drink of water from today onwards, it will come naturally on the day. You can also give yourself a breather by doing a recap of the topic you've just covered: Power Point can be really helpful here, because if you've had a panic and lost your place, your Power Point slide will tell you exactly where you are. Recapping, for your audience and for yourself, will help you to regain control.

Open the floor to questions: if you're confident about your subject, you could invite questions which will change the pace of your presentation, and can enable you to get out of panic mode.

Think about ways of regaining your composure and choose the way or ways that come most easily to you. Practise them frequently in non-threatening situations so that if and when you need them, they're readily available.

Make notes on the following pages about which activities will manage your nervousness best for you.

And don't forget to smile. You're going to be fine.

Your notes

DAY THREE
Produce the goods

*Start feeling the flow and
polishing your presentation*

Right, today's the day we start getting your presentation in order and begin the polishing process. By now, your subconscious will have continued to work on it for you, so you may have some last-minute amendments and additions to make, but by and large you will be ready to pull it all together.

Lots of people come unstuck at this stage because they've never produced a whole presentation in this way, or they're not used to writing.

DAY THREE

A good way to reassure yourself, if you fall into either of these unstuck categories, is to remember that you've been speaking fluently since the age of two or three; that skill is not going to suddenly disappear, so you are perfectly able to put together the words you'll need to make this presentation brilliant.

Consider number three of my Four Laws of Presentations:

1. PREPARE: do your homework on both yourself and your topic

2. PLAN: start with the end in mind. Visualise yourself and your audience having a great time

3. PRODUCE: your speech in its entirety and then as "prompts".

4. PRACTISE: practise, practise and then practise some more

First off, check through your bullet points and the slides that represent them and see if they tell the story you want to tell and make logical sense. Shuffle them around as much as is necessary so that you start to feel a real flow in what you're saying. This "real flow", by the way, feels different for everyone but you'll know it when you get it, rest assured. Take as long as you need.

Complete any research today to back up the subjects you cover, and decide what really adds to the presentation as a whole and what can be left out.

Think about whether you need to expand any of the topics you've identified: do you need to give an example, or illustrate your point or flesh it out in some way?

> **Can you give substance to what you're saying by telling stories that relate to your subject, or would using metaphors bring your subject to life?**

When I asked you to start using visualisation on Day One, for example, I told you stories about Roger Bannister, Jack Canfield and Jack Nicklaus to illustrate my point. While I could simply have explained how visualisation works, I believe you probably gained a clearer understanding of it because of the stories I was able to tell you about it.

DAY THREE

I often talk about body language during my confidence workshops, and I like to ask participants how important they think body language is in creating a first impression. I invite them to guess how much of the first impression you make is down to *what you say*, how much to *how you say it* and how much to *body language*. I write their guesses on a whiteboard and then I click on to my Power Point slide

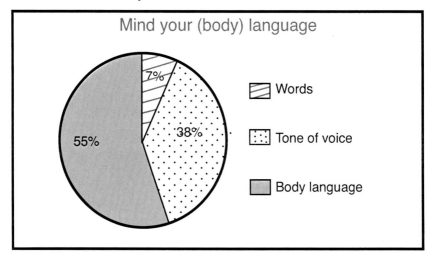

which illustrates my point – both about body language to my workshop participants and about the use of Power Point to you – beautifully. You can use stories and metaphors to drive home the points you think are important. Think also about weeding out any of your bullet points that don't really add value to your presentation. Less is more, remember, especially where presentations are concerned.

Using your bullet points as a framework, practise saying what you need to say, making notes as you go along; stop and start as much as you like, but keep going until you can honestly confirm that you've said everything you need to say.

It's important to work on this stage vocally, just using your bullet points as a framework and **speaking** your script rather than writing it.

> **You will be writing a script shortly, but since your presentation is verbal, I want you to start building it up verbally rather than using only the written word.**

People often write more formally or in a less fluent way than they speak, so it's best to start with speech first, written script next.

If you've written your bullet points on separate piece of paper, it's easy to shuffle them around as you need to until you get the right flow. Because every presentation is different, the content will naturally vary, but you won't go wrong if you follow these

Five golden rules of content

1. **Use simple, familiar words** that you won't trip over. Why say "acclimatise" if you'd usually say "get used to"? Be rigorous about using simple words, even if your subject matter is complicated. You may have no choice but to use unusual or long words, depending on your subject, but you can still keep it simple. Don't use four syllables if two will do.

2. **Keep sentences short and to the point.** Speak as you would normally speak and don't be tempted to use elaborate grammatical constructions. The emphasis up to now has been on speaking your presentation rather than on writing it, and that's because I want you to avoid sounding stilted or convoluted.

3. **Stick with what you know;** if you're not sure about something you need to say, research it thoroughly so that you *are* sure. If you don't feel confident about it, leave it out altogether.

4. Avoid jargon, even if you are presenting to a group that's familiar with your particular lingo – there's always bound to be one person who doesn't understand.

5. Ask yourself what the audience will know when you've finished speaking. If they'll know what you want them to know, you're doing fine and can move on to the next stage. If they won't know what you want them to know, go back and review your bullet points. What else do you need to include? What isn't clear? What needs more research? Can you tell a story or use a metaphor to get part of your message across?

Y ou and your presentation are the focus of this book and of all your efforts at the moment, but it's also important for you to think about your audience's experience. These questions about your subject matter are aimed at helping you to identify ways to satisfy your audience:

Is the purpose of your presentation absolutely clear from the start?

Is your subject matter interesting *and relevant*?

Are you presenting it so that even a child could understand it?

Are you comfortable fielding questions about your subject?

DAY THREE

 Are you giving enough detail to make sense but not so much that your audience is overwhelmed?

 Are you illustrating the main topics with pictures, stories or metaphors?

 Is there an opportunity for the audience to participate in some way?

Focusing on your audience and how they will react to what you're saying will add real power to your presentation, as I reaffirm every time I run a Deep Impact Presentation workshop.

I often ask my workshoppers to get into pairs, one person giving a 90-second presentation, the other giving a 90-second evaluation, and then swapping roles. Everyone gives a presentation, everyone evaluates their partner's presentation.

As well as being good practice, what this little exercise does is illustrate very clearly how focusing on your audience rather than on yourself adds real impact to the presentation.

In every case, the person giving the 90-second presentation is always much less fluent than when they give their 90-second evaluation. So why the marked difference? It's simple: during the presentation, the speaker is focused *inwards*, on their presentation, on their delivery of it, on remembering what they have to say. During the evaluation, by contrast, the presenter is focused *outwards*; they want to make their feedback clear to their partner, so they turn their attention outwards and, as a result, are more relaxed and therefore more fluent.

It's a valuable lesson in how your mindset has a profound effect on the way you act.

While you're thinking about your audience, check that you have some changes of pace, or topic, or activity during the course of your presentation. If it's appropriate and you're sure you'll be able to respond to anything that's thrown at you, could you invite questions? Could you ask your audience a question and use a whiteboard or flip chart to note their responses? If you're delivering a workshop, can you devise an exercise or an activity to illustrate a point?

One very experienced presenter I know regularly invites his audience to get up and change seats. "It's nothing to do with the subject matter," he

DAY THREE

says, "I just don't want people falling asleep!" Asking your audience to change seats may not be appropriate, but think about whether there is a way you could get them moving around so that when they sit down again they're refreshed and fully able to focus on what you want them to know.

When you're happy that you have included everything you want and you've created a good balance between what you say, what your slides show and what you might ask your audience, it's time to write out what you're going to say, word for word.

Take into account the timings you've already considered, and bear in mind that if you want to hold the attention of your audience, you will need to change something every 15 minutes or so: either your pace, your tone, your focus or the mood; ask a question or invite questions or ask if everyone's clear so far, or give your audience exercises or activities to involve them and hold their interest as well as allowing you to add variety.

People tend to remember things in threes, for example Veni Vidi Vici, Churchill's "Blood Sweat and Tears" speech (which was actually Blood, Sweat, Toil and Tears, but is remembered as having only the three key elements), The Good The Bad and The Ugly, Sex Lies and Videotape, and so on. If you can give three examples, or a snappy three-word headline, you'll find it easier to capture your audience's imagination.

This version of your script doesn't have to be a perfect copy because you will probably still want to make changes and, remember, you're going to need to check that your timing is right. All you need for now is all the words on paper. I always advise using large type, at least 18pt or, if you're hand-writing, use a felt tip and double spacing to make what you write easily legible. Put just one paragraph on each separate sheet of paper so that if you want to re-order the presentation it's easily done.

Once you have a script down on paper, give yourself a breather from it. Go and have a cup of coffee or do something else for a half hour or so. When you come back to it, you'll feel refreshed and ready to go.

Now you have the complete script in front of you, and you're well on the way to a brilliant presentation. Right now, what you're going to do is polish it up and make it a perfect fit for you, for the time available and for your audience. At this stage, you'll still need to adjust

DAY THREE

it, add to it or amend it, so read through it several times until you're completely happy with it and are within a minute or so of your target time.

When you're certain you don't need to make any more changes, read through it again, this time in front of a mirror and pausing occasionally to look up at yourself. Do this as many times as it takes to feel comfortable looking up at yourself and away from your script.

> **Read it again. And again. Read it**
> **until you are frankly becoming**
> **just a tiny bit bored with it.**

Read it again, this time using your Power Point slides which will illustrate what you're saying and, if you've prepared them well, will serve as reminders of what you're going to be saying next. Check that the slides don't disrupt your flow: if they do, rejig them and read through again.

Now ask a friend, partner, or simply someone who owes you a favour to listen and watch and, **most importantly**, give you some feedback.

It's surprising how awkward this may feel the first time you do it: it's all a bit full-on, one-to-one, but this is a truly effective way of getting past your nerves. Listen to the feedback and act on it: put right anything that doesn't work, and see if it's possible to do more of what does work. Remember the key question: *what is it you want your audience to know when you've finished speaking?*

Some people find it very difficult to respond to feedback because they feel embarassed about having done something wrong. The healthy approach to your mistakes is to acknowledge them, learn from them and move on. The whole point of asking for feedback is that you want to correct any misunderstandings or mistakes. Please don't waste time and energy by feeling bad about something that isn't quite working; just learn from the feedback, put right whatever was wrong and move on.

Check that your listener knows what you want him to know when you finish your read-through. If he doesn't know, go back to the drawing board, think again about what you need to include and return to the reading through stage until you're ready for another practice rehearsal.

If you've made mistakes, correct them. If your listener doesn't understand something, clarify it. If you've fallen over your words, see if you can simplify that particular sentence or the structure of your sentences in that part of your speech.

DAY THREE

m, just a word about ums. And ers. And any other vocal "tic" you might inadvertently include in your speech. These tics can be absolutely mesmerising as you'll know if you've ever listened to

> **Get good feedback: ask your listener to adopt the "sandwich approach" when they feed back to you on your presentation, that is, they tell you one good thing they noticed, then something not so good, then one more good thing. However helpful your listener wants to be, they won't be helping you at all if they provide only negative feedback, so they need to be prepared to give a rounded critique, not just a blast of criticism. Yes, of course you need to hear the negatives — you're going to correct your mistakes. But you're only human and you need encouragement too.**

someone who peppers their speech liberally with 'um' or 'er' or 'y'know' or 'sorta'. The trouble is, you're mesmerised by the um or er, not the content of the speech.

Using um or er is a lazy way of giving yourself a little time to think of the next thing to say. If you're confident about the next thing to say, you won't need that time. And you will be confident if you follow the exercises and activities in this book. Start noticing and excluding the ums and ers now.

Umming is also a habit that you may have picked up without realising it. While your listener is helping you, ask them to listen to one entire run-through of your presentation doing nothing but counting the tics.

> **You may be surprised by how
> many there are. Once you're
> aware of them, cut them out.**

They don't help you or your presentation and they certainly don't help your audience, so banish them for good.

There's no secret formula for avoiding verbal tics, it's just a question of practising, practising and practising some more, until you don't even hesitate where once you would have ummed.

Time your presentation and adjust it to suit the time you have available. Allow for pauses and at least three deep breaths between each paragraph you deliver. We all tend to speed up when

DAY THREE

we're nervous, so make a conscious effort to slow down, not just when you're timing but of course on the big day, too. While it may seem that taking three deep breaths is way too long a silence, believe that to your audience it will seem like a perfectly natural, relaxed pause, while giving you time to calm any nervousness.

When you feel completely comfortable reading your words aloud, accompanied by the Power Point slides if you're using them, and any visual aids that really make a difference, take a clean sheet of paper and write ONE WORD to represent each paragraph of your speech. If you prefer, you can write each of your one words on a separate postcard.

> **These single words are going to be your**
> **prompts, so all they need to do is remind**
> **you of what you're going to say next.**

You will be using them to replace the full text of your speech over the next day or so, and they will help you to free yourself from the necessity of reading your presentation.

Once you've chosen your single words, check through to make sure you have enough to remind you and not so many that you become entirely dependent on them rather than on your speech.

And that's as much as you need to do on your speech for now. Put it aside, don't think about it any more today.

If you started this book feeling completely terrified of making a presentation and certain that you would make a complete hash of it, I'm guessing there's still some of that unreasoned fear hanging around, despite my best efforts to help you and your own efforts to overcome this unreasoning dread. You're getting there, don't worry, but you probably still feel you have a way to go.

> ### I'm guessing there is a tiny part of you that's saying "this isn't going to work".

There's probably still a voice at the back of your mind saying "I can *never* deliver a good presentation. I've tried before and I *always* fail. It's just one of those things I can't do."

You have had years to build up the idea that you can't do presentations; so you have probably avoided having to do them and, chances are, when you have been unable to escape them, you haven't felt particularly good about what you've done. Your mindset has been "I can't do presentations" and your subconscious has picked up on that idea and run with it.

It has been making sure your belief, your limiting belief, the one that says you can't do presentations, is true. Today's the day to rid yourself forever of that limiting belief and, by the way, any other limiting beliefs that are holding you back. Limiting beliefs can rule our lives and, sometimes, we're not even aware we have them, holding us back and putting boundaries up.

> **Limiting beliefs are the foundation on which most of our negative internal script is based**.

So powerful are these beliefs that we become adept at finding 'evidence' that supports them, thanks in part to what psychologists call the Reticular Activating System, or RAS.

Your RAS is a cluster of brain cells that acts like a radar system, activated by your beliefs or goals. The RAS allows information *in* to your consciousness that is consistent with what you believe (*even if there's no truth in what you believe*), and filters *out* anything that does not support your thoughts, however wrong they are. So again and again, we focus on "evidence" that confirms our limiting belief. Part of our internal script then develops into the reinforcement of these beliefs: "see, I told you I was useless" and "typical, I always do that wrong". RAS and our internal dialogue can create a powerful barrier that limits our ability and scope.

But you can change.

The simple step-by-step plan below will help you to rid yourself of the limiting belief that says you can never deliver a good presentation. (By the way, this process works for every and any limiting belief, so once you've delivered your brilliant presentation, you might want to work through this on any other negative thoughts that hold you back).

Yes, you CAN do it - 1

CLEARLY IDENTIFY YOUR LIMITING BELIEF Because we're so good at hiding the truth about these from ourselves, it's all too easy to overlook them. Clues are in the language you use when it comes to public speaking: I'm hopeless at…   I always mess this up…   I never get this right… I dread doing this… Why does this always go wrong for me…?"

Yes, you CAN do it - 2

ARTICULATE YOUR LIMITING BELIEF Write down what you say when this belief affects your behaviour. When you were asked to make a presentation, for example, did you say (out loud or in your head) something like "Oh, no, don't ask me, I'm terrible" or "That's it, it's all downhill from here"? If you've ever said "I hate speaking in public", or "I just go to pieces as soon as I start to speak if people are watching me", write it down now or write down whatever you usually say about speaking in public or making a presentation. Please don't think too much about it at the moment, just write it down.

Yes, you CAN do it - 3

CROSS THROUGH YOUR LIMITING BELIEF Very therapeutic, this. Don't miss this step: it's a very important one, because it tells your subconscious there's a big change coming in a very visual way. Use a big red felt tip if you have one. Cross through until you push through the paper. Obliterate this limiting belief!

Yes, you CAN do it - 4

ARTICULATE THE EXACT OPPOSITE OF YOUR LIMITING BELIEF Say it in the present tense and in the most positive language you can find. What you say here as the opposite of your limiting belief doesn't necessarily have to be true *at this particular moment*: your subconscious doesn't differentiate between fact and fiction, so "fool" it with the best possible positive spin.

If your limiting belief has been "I can't do presentations" or "I'm terrible at public speaking", make your exact opposite simply " I do presentations really well" or "I love public speaking". Beef it up by saying "I give brilliant presentations" or "I'm a fantastic public speaker". Go for it!

Yes, you CAN do it - 5

WRITE A POSITIVE SCRIPT TO GO WITH YOUR NEW BELIEF Say something like "I enjoy speaking in public and, because I'm so well prepared and rehearsed, my presentations are always brilliant." This step is more effective if you can come up with your own positive script, so have a think about what you really want to say. Go on, say it aloud! Then write it down.

Yes, you CAN do it - 6

ACKNOWLEDGE THIS NEW BELIEF How do you feel now you have this NEW belief about yourself? What does it free you up to do? How does it feel to know that you need never doubt your ability again? Acknowledging your new belief will help to embed it in your psyche. Spend some time getting used to this new belief; remind yourself of it regularly.

Your old, negative belief had lots of time to embed itself, so your subconscious may resist the new, positive belief. Give it a helping hand by really focusing on it now, articulating it, thinking about it, and reminding yourself of it regularly. Write it down, put it on post-it notes wherever you'll see it frequently; read it back to yourself; say it to yourself in the mirror; enlist the help of a friend and say it out loud to them.

Yes, you CAN do it - 7

VISUALISE YOURSELF ACTING ON THIS NEW BELIEF
Your subconscious has been running negative "mini-movies" to
accompany your limiting belief for...who knows how long? Now's
the time to turn the tables and consciously run a mini-movie of
your new *positive* belief. Imagine yourself acting on your new
belief. You created a mini mind movie of yourself delivering a
brilliant presentation on Day One, now run and re-run that movie
again and again until you can summon it up in your mind at will.

Yes, you CAN do it - 8

CREATE AN AFFIRMATION FROM YOUR VISUALISATION The
affirmation you create for yourself will have 100 times more power
than one someone else has given you. When you're able to "switch
on" your visualisation easily and are able to "view" it regularly, write
one or more affirmations to go with it. Make them present tense,
completely positive and in your own voice; something as simple as
"I always deliver brilliant presentations" will work fine. Use words

and phrases you're comfortable with and use in your everyday life. Write your affirmation out and copy it. Make sure you can see it throughout the day and get used to repeating it — you may feel self-conscious at first but that's probably just because your old limiting belief is kicking in. Stick with it, keep reading it, keep saying it. It *will* work.

Work through this superbly positive and effective exercise as often as you like until you can really feel a shift in your thinking.

Banishing limiting beliefs has worked time and time again for my coaching clients, and it will work for you, providing you approach the exercise with an open mind.

You're well on the way now to delivering an absolutely brilliant presentation. Well done you!

Your notes

DAY FOUR

Practice makes perfect

*Rehearse until you can speak
comfortably without notes*

Take a moment to look back to the beginning of the week and give yourself a pat on the back for all you've achieved. If you've been following my day-by-day instructions, by now you will have:

1. Brainstormed your presentation subject matter and applied my Foolproof Presentation Formula to it all.

2. Visualised yourself delivering a first-rate presentation, and you will have become an expert in calling up your positive visualisation.

DAY FOUR

3. Checked out the logistics of your presentation, the venue, the visual aids, what you'll be wearing.

4. Improved your posture so that your body language tells your audience on the Big Day "I'm confident and in control".

5. Practised ways of managing your nervousness.

6. Put together your presentation, following the Five Golden Rules of Content.

7. Practised focusing on your audience and their experience.

8. Delivered your presentation to a selected audience and responded to their feedback.

9. Removed any verbal tics like "ums" and "ers".

10. Banished the limiting belief that said you can't make a brilliant presentation.

Good work so far. Just take a moment to appreciate how much you've already achieved.

*

N ow please take a look at the last of my Four Laws of Presentations, and I'm sure you won't find it difficult to figure out what you're going to be doing from this point onwards:

FOUR LAWS OF PRESENTATIONS

1. **PREPARE:** do your homework on both yourself and your topic

2. **PLAN:** start with the end in mind. Visualise yourself and your audience having a great time

3. **PRODUCE:** your speech in its entirety and then as "prompts".

4. *PRACTISE: practise, practise and then practise some more*

Pick up your speech from yesterday and practise it, with slides if you're using them. Read it through again and again until you're completely comfortable with it. Check that your one-word prompts are appropriate; remember, these one-worders are going to remind you of a complete paragraph or a whole topic in your speech.

Now deliver the whole thing using only your one-word prompts. I'm always ready to pause at this point, while my client gasps and says something like "what? I'm not ready for that. I can't do it! It's too soon."

Then I reassure them that they are, indeed, ready, and I take their written speech away and leave them only with their one-word prompts. If you've followed my directions over the last three days, you ARE ready. If you go on using the script as a crutch any longer, you'll find it even more difficult to let it go, so bite the bullet now.

You'll need to be tough with yourself
at this point and put your script
out of reach.

If you can see it, your dependence on it will have the peculiar effect of making your mind freeze. You'll want that script; you've had a long time telling yourself you can't do this without a script and, if you just put it down in front of you and try to work only from your prompts, you'll find you're irresistibly drawn to the script.

When I'm coaching, I actually take the script away and put it out of sight at this point, usually amid lots of anxious complaints. Trust me, now is exactly the right time to leave your script behind. What will have happened by now, so long as you really have read your speech through at least a dozen times, is that your Power Point slides or visual aids coupled with your one-word prompts will remind you what you need to say next. If they don't, keep reading through until they do. Eventually, you will able to say everything you need to say using only the slides or your one-word prompts to help you.

**If you've ever been in the audience when the
presenter reads the whole presentation, you'll know
why it's so important for you to leave behind
the 'crutch' of your written speech.**

You will be 10 times more convincing and 20 times more interesting if you SPEAK to your audience, rather than reading to them.

In the introduction to this book, I said you'd need about an hour a day for a week to bring you up to speed for making a decent presentation. At this point in the process, only you will know whether an hour is long enough for you to practise. If it's not, be generous: give yourself time enough to feel really comfortable.

Use the visualisation you created on Day One to help you SEE yourself giving an absolutely brilliant presentation; now you've come this far, you can fill in a lot of the blanks and make your

DAY FOUR

mini-movie even more realistic. SEE yourself looking and feeling fantastically confident and in control, happy with your performance. SEE your audience smiling and nodding as you introduce slide number three or four (or whatever number), which illustrates a key piece of information; SEE them watching and listening intently as you summarise all the good stuff you've just said. SEE and HEAR them clapping and thanking you for making the presentation so interesting.

Your visualisation will add to your confidence store every time you use it, and here's another way to give yourself a confidence boost and feel positive at ANY time and especially leading up to your presentation: it's a process called anchoring. If you've ever remembered a particularly happy time and it's made you smile, you've already experienced the most basic form of anchoring.

Anchoring is a way of controlling how you access a positive state using a positive memory. Follow the step-by-step instructions below and try it out for yourself. Some people find it easy to create an anchor while others have to repeat the process two or three times before it works.

Feel positive whenever you want

1. Relax and think back to a really happy memory. Focus on a time in your life when you felt great: confident, full of energy, in control and positive; sportsmen call it being in "the zone", when everything's going well and you feel there's nothing you can't do. Take your time choosing the memory: it needs to be a really upbeat, positive memory with absolutely no negatives attached to it at all.

Once you've identified the memory you're going to use, spend a few minutes really concentrating on it and fleshing it out in your mind. Remember as much detail as you can. How did you feel at the time? Can you conjure up that feeling again? What were you wearing? What kind of day was it? Were you alone or with other people? Try to take yourself right back to that time so you can feel what you felt then, hear the sounds and smell the smells — aroma is one of the most powerful memory stimulants.

How did everything around you look? How did you look? See the scene in the most vibrant brilliant colours possible.

2. Now make the memory even more vibrant in your mind. Concentrate on making your memory as intense as you can, to the point where you *feel* all the good feelings of that time again.

Remember, for your anchor to have the most impact, the memory you use should be completely positive, with no negative undertones. Really concentrate on this memory, making it as vivid and real as it was when you experienced it. At this stage you want to be *feeling* all the feelings you felt at the time, even more strongly than you felt them originally. Some people find this easy, others have to concentrate to get the all-important feelings. It's worth persevering, believe me.

3. Set your anchor. When you are completely immersed in your memory and you're feeling all those lovely positive feelings, you've reached the point at which you can set your anchor. If you have any doubts that you've reached that total immersion stage, focus on the memory again and conjure up the strongest possible feelings until your memory is as real as today's reality.

Then and only then, set your anchor, and give yourself a physical signal to trigger this wonderful memory. Some people like to imagine a "save" button they can click in their palm; you could squeeze your thumb and forefinger together, or tap your wrist, or push your hair behind your ears, or whatever action comes easily to you.

4. Come back to reality. You're going to test your anchor in a moment, but for now, you need to come back to the present, and you can do this by simply counting backwards from 295 to 289. Notice how you're now focused on what's happening at this moment.

5. Trigger your anchor. Test your trigger by hitting your save button in your palm or pinching your thumb and finger together — use whatever physical signal you decided on in Step Three, and you should be immediately flooded with the good feelings you had at the time of your original memory. You won't have to think about it or try to recall the memory you used — triggering the anchor you've set should be enough to automatically create the mindset you had in your memory.

If it doesn't happen, go back to the beginning and try to focus even more forcefully on the memory, make it even more vivid and loud and be sure you're experiencing the feelings you felt at the time.

Anchoring works really well, and will give you an inestimable advantage if you use it before your presentation because you will start out feeling confident, calm and happy.

Practise using your trigger and enjoying the anchoring experience from today onwards, so that on the Big Day you can access your confident, calm, happy state easily.

Once you've set one anchor, there's no limit to the number you can set, so long as you remember the golden rules: use a different trigger for each anchor and make them all completely positive and as vivid as possible.

Your notes

Your notes

DAY FIVE

Are you nearly ready?

*Make sure you're giving yourself
the best possible start*

Today is the day for a dress rehearsal. Wear what you're going to wear, recreate the real thing as closely as possible and run through your presentation, noticing any glitches and putting them right.

At this stage, we're not looking for major changes, just tweaks and minor adjustments. Is there a place where you always stumble or forget the next thing you need to say, for example? If so, change the words or change the order so you iron out the stumble and can move on without drying

DAY FIVE

up. Does the Power Point make complete sense and does it really add to what you're saying? It's surprising how often, at this stage, my clients realise that they have included too many slides or that some of them just aren't adding anything worthwhile. Less is more, remember.

Do you feel comfortable in the clothes you're wearing? If not, change them or make whatever adjustments are needed to make them right. The way you look is completely unimportant, actually — *just as long as the way you look doesn't grab your audience's attention so much that they can't or don't concentrate on what you're saying.*

They'll only focus on you if your look is wildly inappropriate or dishevelled.

Think about the last time you attended a presentation: after initially checking out the way the presenter looked, your focus was on what they said rather than on how they looked. You don't need to be a fashion plate. You simply need to be wearing an outfit that's appropriate for the subject matter, the audience and the venue, and you need to feel comfortable wearing it.

You need to look well groomed and ready. When you've created that look, you can forget about your appearance entirely on the day and focus your attention on your audience.

After a solo run-through, add the extra detail of an audience, either the same friend or partner as before, or someone new. Ask the all-important question: at the end of the presentation do they know what you wanted them to know?

Listen to their feedback and make whatever changes are necessary to address their comments or criticisms. If you can't find someone to help you out, try speaking into a recorder or if you have webcam let your trusty computer be a substitute audience. Leave a gap between recording and viewing and then try to be completely detached when you view your efforts back.

C hecking the logistics of your presentation is also important today, and by that I mean confirm with the venue that everything you need is available and working, and check your travel time to the venue. Most people need a projector and laptop, and a lectern for any visual aids or one-word prompts you may use. You might need specific

DAY FIVE

equipment relevant to your presentation and it's worth double-checking that everything you need is there on the day and working.

If you're not good with technology, it's also important to ask if there will be someone on hand who can help out with any problems with connectivity. There's nothing more frustrating or off-putting than having every bit of equipment you need but not knowing where the on/off switch is!

Is the room laid out the way you want? Is there enough room for you to move around? Is there a table or desk at the side of your space where you can put your visual aids and a jug and glass of water?

How long is it going to take you to reach the venue?

**Think in terms of arriving one hour
before your presentation
is due to begin.**

You want time to make sure all the equipment's working, the room is laid out as you want and, more than anything, you want time to deal with the unexpected. An hour may seem like a long time, but that hour gives you the reassurance of knowing you can prepare for every eventuality. One of my clients tells the story of arriving 20 minutes before he was due to deliver a keynote speech at a conference; plenty of time, you'd think. But the laptop provided for him died as it was switched on. Finding another available laptop, connecting it up and getting it ready meant he not only had no time for a final read-through, he was late starting and felt anxious for the first 15 minutes of his speech.

> **"I knew that speech like the back of my hand," he told me, "but sorting out the problem with the laptop really threw me."**

"Instead of having a last read-through, I was running around trying to find the right connection lead. Right up to the last minute, I didn't know if we'd get the thing properly connected to the projector, so I kept trying to revise what to say to compensate for the lack of Power Point. We did get it working, but it took me 15 minutes to get into my stride. My speech didn't have the impact it should have had and it shook my confidence."

If you think your travel time is one hour, leave two hours before you're due to start; if your travel time is two hours, leave at least three and a half hours before you're due to start. This may sound over-generous, but wouldn't you prefer to get there in plenty of time, have a cup of tea, read the paper, really relax, read through your notes perhaps? Much better

DAY FIVE

arrive with too much time to spare than get there all in a panic and have to start your presentation feeling not quite ready.

A note on your audience. As well as practising today, please fix this thought in your mind: your audience will want you to succeed.

I say this not because I know every audience is good-hearted and generous, but because I know every audience consists of people who don't want to have to feel sorry for a bumbling fool.

If your presentation is good, they'll enjoy it and take in your message. If it's awful and you're a nervous stuttering mess, they're not only unlikely to enjoy it, they'll also struggle to remember what you wanted to convey. Remember this when you look at your audience: it's in their interest for you to do well. They're rooting for you!

Browse through the tried and tested confidence boosters below and start using the ones you like now, today. Some may resonate with you more than others. That's fine, just pick the ones with which you feel most comfortable and which you feel will have the most impact on you and USE THEM. Start today — don't leave it until you're in dire need.

Confidence boosters galore

1. Write yourself a winner's script If you've worked through the limiting beliefs exercise on Day Three, you will already have a winner's script, so review and refine it now. If you go into a challenging situation with a little voice at the back of your mind saying "you KNOW you're going to mess up; you're USELESS at this; you ALWAYS get this sort of thing WRONG", the chances are you will mess up, be useless and get it wrong.

The most effective winner's script is the one you write for yourself. Write it and repeat it often; make it short and sweet so it will fit on post-it notes on your monitor, on your bedside table, in your wallet or purse, anywhere that you'll see it throughout the day.

2. SEE yourself successful Run your mini-movie, the one you created from your visualisation on Day One, regularly. Make it bright and clear; make it brighter and clearer, more and more vivid; HEAR it as well as seeing it; FEEL it. Repeat as required until you can switch it on in your mind as often and as easily as breathing.

3. Analyse a winner Think of someone you know who always seems confident and self-assured. Think of that person giving a presentation. How would they speak?

How would they stand? What would they wear? What would they expect to happen? How would they prepare? Once you've analysed your winner's methods, steal them!

If they speak slowly and clearly, do the same. If they stand tall with good posture, do the same; will you wear something that is comfortable and appropriate, will you have a positive expectation, be well prepared?

4. Remember you're a winner If you've successfully set an anchor, you're already on your way, but this is a slightly different and incredibly powerful way of using your inner resources. Think back to a time when you felt successful and completely confident: it could be yesterday, last week, last year or two decades ago.

The feeling may have lasted two minutes or two years. It doesn't matter when or where it was or how long it lasted, what matters is how you felt.

Think back to that feeling; concentrate on the way you felt at that time. Think about it, how you felt, how you carried yourself, how you looked, what you said or did while you felt so confident.

Why were you so successful and confident? What had you achieved that gave you that feeling? What were you doing? How did other people respond to you? Really see yourself as you were then, when you felt successful and confident. Get a very clear picture in your mind. Now imagine that successful, confident you delivering your presentation.

5. Be kind to yourself Imagine you are able to clone yourself. Picture a you2 standing right in front of you. Now tell that you2 how great you are; praise your you2's achievements and efforts; tell your you2 you have faith in them; you believe in your you2 and you know they will succeed. Finally, give your you2 a big hug and

DAY FIVE

concentrate on letting him or her know how much you care about them and believe in them. Some people find this works better for them if they picture themselves as a child; others find they respond better to an adult clone — it's up to you. Give it a try.

6. Smile a lot more, not just for this presentation but all the time: when you walk down the street, when you meet people. Generally look happier even if you're not feeling that way.

7. Learn from the past; don't beat yourself up about it. It's gone; it's never coming back. Instead, learn from it for next time.

8. Prepare for every possible situation, as much as is practical. Think through what you plan to do, and visualise as clearly as possible how you want things to work. Try to notice where problems might arise, and deal with them in good time.

9. Play to your strengths. Know what you are good at and expose yourself to the possibility of using them at every opportunity – because you're good at it, you'll enjoy it and have more confidence. This is especially important when you're facing a challenge: whenever you take a break from the challenge, give yourself a chance to excel at something else!

10. Refuse to be inferior. Eleanor Roosevelt used to say: "No one can make you feel inferior without your consent." And of course she was right.

Your notes

DAY SIX

Practise makes perfect

*Run through until you feel confident
then sit back and relax*

onsider number 4 of my Four Laws of Presentations over the page
and it's obvious what you're going to be doing today! You've read
through and run through your presentation so many times by now
that you have created neural pathways in your brain to accommodate it.
So your run-throughs today should be laid-back and low-key. Nice and
easy and relaxed.

Check through your one-word prompts and make sure they're in good

FOUR LAWS OF PRESENTATIONS

1. PREPARE: do your homework on both yourself and your topic

2. PLAN: start with the end in mind. Visualise yourself and your audience having a great time

3. PRODUCE: your speech in its entirety and then as "prompts".

4. PRACTISE: practise, practise and then practise some more

order; make sure too that they still provide the reminders you need in the order you need them.

Remember to pause for breath before every new paragraph you say. Smile as you pause — don't fake it, you will be feeling relaxed enough now to smile. Every subject, except perhaps the gloomiest of announcements, will be enhanced by a smile. You won't be making any changes today — you won't need to. You don't need to do a rehearsal in front of an audience today. But you do need to say your presentation to yourself in front of a mirror. Doing this will confirm and endorse all the practice you've been doing.

Some people find this final mirror rehearsal the most difficult of all, but it's worth persevering. You've already done it once on Day Three and this last mirror rehearsal will really help you to iron out any self-consciousness or remnants of anxiety. Run through your presentation as many times as you need to, in front of a mirror, until you feel completely relaxed about it. Then stop. Your presentation is ready.

oday's a good time to practise some of the relaxation techniques from Day Two. And here's the ultimate relaxation tool: The Golden Room, a perfect place of peace and tranquillity you can visit whenever you like. When the shark bites, when the bee stings, when you're feeling sad or when you're beginning to feel incredibly nervous about your presentation, simply transport yourself to a beautiful place where everything is exactly as you want it to be.

It's all in the mind, of course, but this exercise in visualisation gives you a personal retreat to which you can retire if ever the world becomes just a bit too hard to bear.

This is where you relax

There are many variations on this theme — I've heard of a version that native Americans use, one that's popular with hypnotherapists, and yet another that was passed on to me by a friend who'd heard it at her church.

This is my own version, and it works fantastically well for me and my clients. Give it a try, and if you find you need to add details or change the ambiance, fine — it will work better for you if you have created it for yourself.

Imagine a cube, about 10ft x 10ft x 10ft. This cube is made up of bright, golden light which gives off a gentle warmth. This cube is the Golden Room. Give yourself a minute or so to really picture this room: it is bounded only by light, and everything you place in it is bathed in beautiful clear rays of energy. My Golden Room contains a sofa with comfortable cushions that are soft as thistledown; there is a lavender aroma; I can occasionally hear wind chimes in the distance, and I often hear the shushing sound of the sea lapping against a sandy beach.

You will choose your own details: your Golden Room may contain only clouds or a simple table and chair; there may be no aroma, or it may be the delicious fragrance of an apple pie cooking in the oven in your mum's kitchen; your Golden Room may have beautiful pictures or sculptures or books — it's entirely up to you.

Fill your Golden Room with things and sensations that bring you pleasure and comfort.

Because this Golden Room is entirely yours, you can have fountains of liquid silver or baby deer, tame tigers or gleaming cars — there's no limit to what you can have, except that whatever you choose must bring you pleasure and comfort.

Your Golden Room may be minimalist or you might go for Art Deco or Goth or something that only you could describe. Great! Enjoy the experience of creating this light-filled space exactly as you want it to be.

This Golden Room, once you've described it clearly and fully to yourself, is where you will go when you need to relax, or take time out, or move away from a stressful situation. The bright golden light in your Golden Room will fill you with a feeling of calm and peace; your energy reserves will be topped up by it; aches and pains will be relieved by it.

> **Tears that you take to the Golden Room**
> **evaporate in the gentle warmth of the light,**
> **leaving you feeling refreshed and revived.**

Sadness seeps away in the Golden Room; anger dissipates and tension simply disappears. Now see yourself in the Golden Room.

Notice how relaxed and calm you are. Notice how happy you feel; acknowledge that while you're there, nothing troubles you.

Realise how clearly you are able to think while you're here. Feel how much the light refreshes you, re-energises you and gives you a sense of comfort and security.

Once you have a Golden Room of your own, you can go there whenever you need a boost of energy or confidence, or respite from stress. It's a great place to go when you feel unhappy or sad, or when your temper's getting the better of you.

> If you're feeling nervous a few seconds in the Golden Room can calm you down; the train journey home can be a little piece of heaven if you concentrate on spending your time in the Golden Room instead of in a crowded carriage. You can visit as often as you like and stay as long as you like, and you can add or subtract from what's inside it. The only thing that's constant is the bright golden light and the feeling it promotes of calm and refreshment. Beyond that, the only limit is your own imagination.

A minute or two in your Golden Room before you deliver your presentation will help you to feel relaxed, energised, calm and in control. Enjoy!

Your notes

Your notes

Your notes

DAY SEVEN

Well done, you're ready to roll

*All you need to do today is remind
yourself that you believe in you*

You've made it! You've put in a huge amount of hard work over
the last week, and now you've reached The Big Day, the day you
deliver your presentation. You're ready, don't worry, but there are
still one or two things you can do today to give yourself an edge.

First of all, look over your notes and your Power Point presentation.
Check through your one-word prompts, if you're using them. Today

DAY SEVEN

you should aim at having just one or two run-throughs of the whole presentation: please don't allow anxiety to force you into a frantic rehearsal session on the day. There's no point and no need. You're ready.

Consciously slow yourself down as you run through your presentation; your nerves will probably prompt you to speed up, but stay in control. Breathe deeply between each paragraph and concentrate on regulating your speed to the point where you feel you're going too slowly. You definitely won't be.

Here's your final checklist:

 What time do you need to set off to arrive with an hour to spare? Make sure your timing's spot on today.

 Once you've run through your presentation a couple of times, put it to one side. Put your notes, your one-word prompts and any visual aids ready to take with you when you leave. You don't need rushed rehearsals today. *You're ready.*

 Run your mind movie, the one you created on Day One and have revisited several times. Take as much time as you need to recreate it really vividly. See yourself, completely calm and in control, delivering a spectacularly good presentation. See the audience giving you a standing ovation at the end. Feel how great it is to have achieved this.

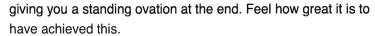 Remind yourself of the calming exercises you did on Day Two: which will you use today? They will all be useful, especially if you've been practising them regularly.

Repeat the affirmations you created on Day Three when you banished your limiting belief, the one that claimed you were hopeless at presentations. Use them as a mantra today; they'll help to calm and focus you.

Use the anchor you set on Day Four to give yourself a really good positivity booster. Remember to use your smile, too — your smile is a great anchor and, even if you fake it, will give you an endorphin boost.

Use as many of the confidence boosters from Day Five as you need, as many times as you like.

Take a final look in the mirror: you're looking well groomed and you feel comfortable in what you're wearing. Great, now forget about the way you look.

When you arrive at the venue, take time to visit your Golden

Room visualisation so that you give yourself a peaceful, calming space before you start.

You may feel nervous today even though, if you've worked through all the exercises and activities in this book, you really are ready. Remember, your nervousness is your body's way of helping you to prepare for the big event.

Acknowledge that it's good to feel nervous and know you can deal with it: your body is preparing you to meet a challenge, one for which you are extremely well prepared both physically and psychologically. The nervousness you feel will help you to rise to the occasion, so don't be afraid of it; USE it to help you to excel.

The simplest way to ground yourself is to use the deep breathing exercises you learned on Day Two. They are easy to do, and will help you to regain and maintain your composure.

And so will knowing that you've done all you possibly can to make this presentation brilliant.

Remember to slow down and smile. Trust yourself and all the preparation you've done. Remember, too, the all-important fact that is sometimes overlooked among all the preparation and rehearsal: your audience wants you to succeed.

And check out these last-minute hot tips to help keep your confidence high and ensure your presentation is brilliant:

Final confidence boosters

1. **Remind** yourself of all the beautiful preparation you've done over the last week and what it means: that you're really ready.

2. **Befriend your nerves.** Acknowledge that you're nervous, accept that everyone, even the most experienced public speaker, gets nervous and harness your nervousness in a positive way. Visualise yourself making your speech and "see" the audience responding warmly to everything you say, applauding and cheering. Visualise a torrent of cheering and thunderous applause as you take your leave. Do whatever needs to be done to ensure that your nerves are under control on the day. Use the ideas from Day Two and practise your most effective calmers often.

3. **Fake it till you make it.** Think of the most brilliant speaker

you've ever seen and copy them. It's called modelling, and it works. If no-one springs to mind, simply stand tall, as though there's a string at the top of your head pulling you gently upwards, pull your shoulders back and push your chest out. Smile. Your body language gives powerful signals not only to the world around you, but to your own subconscious, so make sure your posture is upright and open. Act confidently and you will feel confident.

4. Talk yourself up. Psychologists say we all have an internal dialogue (some of us actually say it out loud too) and around 55,000 thoughts a day. A staggering 80% of this internal dialogue and our thoughts is negative. Offset this negative bombardment by focusing on the positive: have an affirmation that says something like "I've prepared really well for this and I'm going to enjoy it" or "Everyone wants me to succeed and I'm going to do just that". Remember, the affirmation or mantra you create for yourself will be the most powerful – so long as you repeat it frequently.

5. Look outward, not inward. Focus on your surroundings and your audience rather than on yourself. Notice the size or shape of the room, the number of chairs, people coming in; find someone with a friendly face and focus on him or her. If it's viable, welcome people as they arrive. Focus on their needs, not yours. In fact, focus on anything at all, so long as you're not focusing on you and how nervous you feel.

6. Breathe. Use deep breathing to pull in as much oxygen as you can. Your brain, though not your largest organ, uses up to 20% of all the oxygen available to your body, so ensure your thinking cap is fully oxygenated. Adrenalin, the fight or flight hormone, causes breaths to become shallow, or may even prompt you to hold your breath. Deep breathing will help your brain work more efficiently, and taking control of your breathing rate is calming.

7. Drink plenty of water. One of the first things to happen when you become nervous is that your mouth goes dry, so hydrate at every opportunity. Taking a sip of water before you start to speak also gives you a few extra vital seconds to take control and calm yourself.

8. Massage your forehead. Adrenalin sends blood to the fight/ flight centres of your brain which are at the base of your skull. Put your fingers on your forehead and massage gently on the bony parts, to help bring the blood to the frontal lobes, the parts of the brain that are engaged when you are speaking.

9. Use your imagination. Look out at your audience and imagine them all stark naked. It will make you smile, and break through the worst of your nervousness. Follow this up quickly with a vision of your audience cheering and clapping as you complete your presentation. They can be clothed or unclothed, whichever works best for you!

10. Fast forward 10 years. If you do forget a point or fluff a pronunciation, will it really matter? You're highly unlikely to mess up because you're so well prepared.

Start out being determined to enjoy the experience, have confidence in the excellent preparation you've done, and go for it.

Good luck!

And finally...

You've done it! You've overcome your unreasoning fear and, perhaps, a long-held limiting belief and delivered a presentation that was brilliant. And it now forms the basis for a great template from which you can work on your next presentation.

Now's the time to look back at what you did well and what didn't work so well, where you felt perfectly comfortable and where, perhaps, you struggled or felt as though you were losing it.

You've broken through the fear barrier, and it's important now to review your achievement and, honestly, see where you can improve. I have no doubt it was brilliant but even the most brilliant presentations can be improved. The most successful speakers and presenters are the

And finally

ones who are rigorous and consistent about reviewing and evaluating, improving and upgrading.

It's also important to get some feedback from those who heard and saw your presentation and, of course, it's equally important that you respond to that feedback by revelling in all the praise and relishing your success as well as correcting what didn't work so well. Every presentation you deliver is an opportunity to learn more, improve your technique and develop a truly consistently brilliant style.

And now you've so successfully banished your glossophobia, who knows which other areas of your life you might start developing? Sucess is eminently transferable and I hope you'll feel ready to bring that same winning feeling to other parts of your life you want to improve.

Please let me know at hazel@redbirdcoaching.co.uk how well you do. I love success stories!

Hazel Walker

redbird coaching

Tried and tested
ways to find your mojo
and keep it working at full tilt

YOUR ONE-WEEK COUNTDOWN TO BRILLIANT MOTIVATION

by Hazel Walker

www.**red**birdcoaching.co.uk

DAY ONE

What lights your fire?

Make sure you have the right kind of fuel
to keep your motivation fire burning bright

My two children are as different as chalk and cheese and, despite my vows to treat them equally, I quickly discovered I had to adopt different tactics to motivate my son to those I used to motivate my daughter.

My daughter, the first-born, usually responded to a simple carrot: *do this*, I'd say, *and you'll get that reward*, and she would respond more or less consistently. Yes, she wanted that reward so she would go all out to do whatever I asked. When my son arrived I soon realised he was a much less simple kettle of fish. Occasionally he would go for the carrot but mostly he liked to decide on his own rewards and motivators. I could persuade him into action only if I could convince him that it was his own idea, that doing whatever it was I wanted him to do would please him and give him a feeling of satisfaction.

In simple terms, you could say my daughter responded to external drivers, while my son responded only to internal drivers.

You may recognise yourself in one or other of these categories but you may equally swing between the two, depending on what you're doing.

Now my children are fully grown adults with their own fully developed personalities and, just as when they were little, their motivators are different. What rocks my daughter's boat won't motivate my son, and vice versa. They both have clearly defined values, which help them when it comes to making major life decisions and staying motivated.

And the simple fact is, whether they're internally or externally driven, they're much more likely to stay motivated if what they're doing aligns with their values. My daughter discovered this the hard way when she took her first job which gave her a good salary but absolutely no job satisfaction.

Within a month she was bored brainless and couldn't wait to hand in her notice.

My son, on the other hand, has quite often worked in jobs that haven't inspired him at all but have rewarded him well financially – so long as he has an end in sight, that is, something on which he wants to spend his hard-earned dosh! Different as ever.

There's no right or wrong in terms of values. What you feel is important, your gut instinct, is right for you.

And while some people manage to go through their whole lives without ever consciously analysing their values, I believe if you want to stay motivated enough to achieve your goals, you need to know and understand your values so that you can make sure your efforts are in line with them.

If you can identify your core life values right away, great. Jot them down because we'll be working with them over the coming days and they will affect your decisions and your motivation. If you can't articulate your values straight away or they don't immediately spring to mind, here are some exercises to help you in identifying them.

Use all three if you like, or read through and then just go for the one that resonates most with you.

What are your values? – 2

This exercise sounds bleak, but it really isn't: simply imagine your own funeral. Imagine who will be there, the individuals and the *kind of people* who will attend.

Now imagine that every person there will have the opportunity to stand up and speak about you. What will they say?

If you find this difficult to visualise, try thinking about what you'd *like* them to say – the two may not be the same.

From what your family friends and loved ones say about you, or from what you'd *like* them to say about you, you will begin to get a clear view of what your true values are.

What are your values? – 2

i. Think about the three happiest, most successful times in your life. You may have one or two, or many to choose from; if need be, whittle down your choices by making sure your good memories reflect times when you felt not only happy, but also satisfied, secure, and at ease with yourself. Make sure your memory is entirely positive, with no negative input at all.

ii. From the list below – which isn't comprehensive by any means, so feel free to add to it – choose the values that were uppermost in your mind at those happiest times. You may find this difficult to do, so don't rush it. When you've created your own list of selected values, prioritise it by comparing the values in pairs and deciding which of the two is most important to you. Keep doing this until you are left with no more than a dozen key values.

You may have many values that are not yet listed here, so please feel free to add and amend as necessary. You might also find, as you work through this book, that new ideas and thoughts on values come to you. That's fine, jot them down on the pages provided for your notes. Remember, this list is not definitive and is intended only to help to kickstart your thinking:

Abstinence, Accountability, Achievement, Adventure, Ambition, Approval, Art, Assertiveness, Balance, Beauty, Boldness, Calmness, Carefulness, Challenge, Charity, Cheerfulness, Clear conscience, Commitment, Community, Compassion, Consistency, Contentment, Control, Cooperation, Courtesy, Creativity, Decisiveness, Dependability, Determination, Diligence, Discipline, Discretion, Dynamism, Economy, Efficiency, Elegance, Empathy, Enjoyment, Enthusiasm, Equality, Excellence, Excitement, Exploration, Fairness, Faith, Family, Fitness, Fluency, Focus, Freedom, Friends, Fun, Generosity, Goodness, Grace, Growth, Happiness, Hard Work, Harmony, Health, Honesty, Honour, Humility, Independence, Ingenuity, Inquisitiveness, Insight, Intelligence, Intellect, Intuition, Irreverence, Joy, Justice, Kindness, Leadership, Love, Loyalty, Mastery, Monogamy, Obedience, Order, Originality, Perfection, Positivity, Power, Practicality, Professionalism, Reliability, Religion, Restraint, Results, Security, Sensitivity, Serenity, Simplicity, Spontaneity, Thoroughness,

Thoughtfulness, Tolerance, Traditions, Trustworthiness, Truth, Valour, Wealth, Zeal.

iii. When you've identified your top values, put them in order. This can be a challenge, especially if you haven't given much thought to your values for a while.

Thinking about what you could set aside will help you to weed out any less important values; thinking about which values would mean most in life-or-death situations also helps. This exercise is aimed at getting you back in touch with your real self, so expect to do some hard thinking.

What are your values? – 3

Ask yourself these power questions. Getting to your answers will require you to dig deep and will trigger lots of thoughts about what your real values are:

1. What do you want to accomplish before you die?
2. What is the first change you would make on the way to accomplishing your dream?
3. What do you need MORE of in your life?

DAY ONE

4. What do you need LESS of in your life?
5. If you had to guess your life purpose, what would it be?
6. What action would you take if you knew you could not fail?

Finally, once you've clearly identified your values, think about what you want to achieve, and decide whether your activities are in line with your values. Where there's alignment, your motivation will be high and you'll maintain your momentum; where your activities and your values are not aligned, you'll find it difficult to stay motivated or even to make a start, because you'll be fighting yourself every inch of the way.

You can often find ways of making your activities align with your values, just by giving them some thought. It's worth it, because a mismatch between your values and what you do will always be a drain on your energy and your motivation.

For more help with getting your mojo back, YOUR ONE-WEEK COUNTDOWN TO BRILLIANT MOTIVATION is available at www. redbirdcoaching.co.uk and good bookshops from July 2011.